THE WAY WE LIVE

THE WAY WE LIVE

KATHLEEN JAMIE

BLOODAXE BOOKS

ISBN: 1 85224 034 2

First published 1987 by
Bloodaxe Books Ltd,
P.O. Box 1SN,
Newcastle upon Tyne NE99 1SN.

Bloodaxe Books Ltd acknowledges
the financial assistance of Northern Arts.

Typesetting by Bryan Williamson, Manchester

Printed in Great Britain by
Bell & Bain Limited, Glasgow, Scotland.

For Andrew

Acknowledgements

Acknowledgements are due to the editors of the following publications in which some of these poems have appeared: *Blind Serpent, The Literary Review, London Magazine, Making for the Open* (Chatto & Windus, 1985) *New Writing Scotland II, Orbis, Paper, Poetry Book Society Anthology 1987/88* (PBS/Hutchinson, 1987), *Poetry Durham,* and *Prospice.* Four of the poems were published in *Black Spiders* by Kathleen Jamie (Salamander Press, 1982). 'Emotion is human' and 'That day was raised' were broadcast on *A Sense of Place* (BBC Radio 4).

Kathleen Jamie wishes to thank the Scottish Arts Council for a Writer's Bursary awarded in 1985.

Contents

I.

Clearances

The wind sucks clouds. In the indrawn breath
grass bends and nods, like Mandarins.
The sun hunches, and begins to set no sooner
than it's risen. This
depopulated place! Where moorland birds
repeat a sound, like copper, beaten.
The very moon imagines things –
a desert dusk, with itself as scimitar...
As the wind keeps up, closer than
I've heard my name in...how long?
and the dark coheres; an old idea
returns again, the prodigal friend:
of leaving: for Szechwan, or Persia.

Bosegran

Everything is natural, from the cotton summer
dress to the horizon; a natural illusion.
In the water of the cove, with its plates
of green weed fixed and shifting like continents,
is some irritation – an object discarded from a boat
or the few white houses on the shore
looking out to sea. The sea lies open as an eye.

Alone in all the world one is playing.
A seal, fluid and dark, has the plastic colonised,
round her like a jacket. I watched them tumble
and dive, and water cuff rock
till the sea took the colour of the sky. To what end?
– but 'why?' is just salt blown in the mind's eye.
The seal delights. The sun climbs higher as the world goes about.

Poem for a departing mountaineer

Regarding the skyline longingly
(curved as a body, my own, I desire you)
where ink-coloured cloud masses
and rolls on the ridge,
I pick out silhouettes. Deer
dolmen, trees, perhaps tombs
raised through the bracken and weird
midsummer nights by the ancients.
Or men. I can't discern, and mustn't wonder
whether the figures are vibrant, stone,
setting out hunched under loads
or turning home. I must be distant,
draw the curtains for bed,
and leave them, like you who left
with your grave-goods strapped to your back
alone to the lowering cloud.

November

He can touch me with a look
as thoughtless as afternoon
and think as much of hindering me
as he would of sailing away.

In November, when the storms come
he drums his fingers on his books and turns
them into a fist that crashes. On the shore
where he insists we walk, he holds me like a man
at a deck-rail in a gale. I suspect his eyes
are open, red and gazing over my head
in the direction of abroad.

I am left to tell him in a voice that
seems as casual as his talk of travel:
I think as much of leaving as
of forcing him to stay.

Duet

I am the music of the string duet
in the Métro, and my circumstances,
nowadays, are music too: travelling
the underground like women's scent, or happiness.
Again and again I discover that I love you
as we navigate round Châtelet
and hear once more the music. It's found its way
through passages to where I least expect,
and when you kiss me, floods me.
The trains come in, whine out again,
the platforms fill and empty:
a movement regular as your heart's
beat, mine as lively as the melody.

Julian of Norwich

Everything I do I do for you.
Brute. You inform the dark
inside of stones, the winds draughting in

from this world and that to come,
but never touch me.
You took me on

but dart like a rabbit into holes
from the edges of my sense
when I turn, walk, turn.

*

I am the hermit whom you keep
at the garden's end, but I wander.
I am wandering in your acres

where every step, were I
attuned to sense them,
would crush a thousand flowers.

(Hush, that's not the attitude)
I keep prepared a room and no one comes.
(Love is the attitude)

*

Canary that I am, caged and hung
from the eaves of the world
to trill your praise.

He will not come.
Poor bloodless hands, unclasp.
Stiffened, stone-cold knees, bear me up.

(And yet, and yet, I am suspended
in his joy, huge and helpless
as the harvest moon in a summer sky.)

The barometer

Last year
Mother threw the barometer
the length of the corridor. This:
she has set her jaw. There's a chill
and the rustle of weeds. She's come in
from the garden, now she'll withdraw.

The maids are shivering. Outside
they're talking of snow. I say no
to a fire – it's an act of surrender.

I can see the bare fields from here
on the balcony. The nights
are growing longer. I know.
At least the harvest is gathered and safe.
– Every thanksgiving
I dance like a Romany. Indian summers;
I giggle and weep. Mother and me
go picnics in the blossoming...

My furs are laid out and waiting.
The maids keep tutting.
I catch myself biting
dead skin from my lips.
I have played with my gloves all day.

I ought just to jump
and meet Hades half way.

Black spiders

He looked up to the convent
she'd gone to. She answered no questions
but he knew by the way she'd turned away
that morning.
He felt like swimming to the caves.

*

The nuns have retreated. The eldest still
peals the bell in glee, although no one comes
from the ruins. All their praying was done
when they first saw the ships and the Turks'
swords reflecting the sun.

In the convent the cistern is dry,
the collection boxes empty – cleft skulls
severed and bleached,
are kept in a shrine, and stare to the East.

*

She caught sight of him later, below, brushing salt
from the hair of his nipples. She wanted them
to tickle; black spiders on her lips.

Lepidoptery

So you stay
up at night mounting angels
you've caught
on the leaves of a book,
arranging the wings
in precise (be honest,
lifeless) imitations of flight.

You prefer the
perfect collection.
Most angels are mortal;
they look vague
and benign, as sexlessness ought.

We should pity
the fluttering creatures
who gamble their lives for
a chance to be
shadows, however frantic and huge.

Real angels laugh
in the presence of light.
They can taste ether
high on the wind.

I want one of those,
the immortals, the
threatening, true,
proclamatory angels, the blinding,
the kind lusted after by
equinox gales. I
dream of sustaining one, breathing.

Peter the Rock

The last trumpet of sunlight blows over the sea,
he moves high on the cliff, sure of his grace
and raises an arm. The fingers connect.
He pulls up and leans out, hair falling straight toward earth.

He tells me he dreams about nothing
but falling, though we sleep on the sand.
His arms always round me, golden hair
spilled over my face. That mysterious injury
torn in his shoulders: 'I told you, I fell.'

Even in kissing you feel for holds,
grip through to bone.
It doesn't surprise me, I do it myself,
enrage you with symbol, the meaning of things.
You practise moves and hate gestures,
God-talk with vengeance, imperfect shoulders.

I change the tapes. He drives, and will go on denying
into the night. There is nothing
but rock and the climbing of rock under the sun.
Which I say is falling and setting behind us, unfolded,
flashed in the wing mirrors, golden, your skin tone.

Permanent cabaret

Our highwire artiste,
knowing nothing of fear, will take
sparkling risks fifty feet high.
Her costume, ladies, is iced with
hard diamonds.
While she mounts all those steps
our old friend the clown will stand
upside down in a shower of confetti
and chirp 'Love me!'

Their lamp is the last on camp to go out.
Coco reads Jung, sometimes aloud to
Estelle, if she's sewing on sequins.
More often she practises alone in the ring
for the day she enters permanent cabaret,
perhaps in Zurich. Coco cracks his knuckles,
thinking vaguely of children, or considers
repainting the outside of their van.

Half way across Estelle glitters like frost.
She has frozen. 'Remain professional.' She
draws breath through her teeth, wavers
her hand: 'Let Coco sense something for once!'
His red boots are edging towards her. He
coaxes, offers aid – his absurd umbrella. ·
The audience wonder: is it part of the show
this embarrassing wobbling,
this vain desperation to clutch?

The belt

Then he said 'Yes, there's another,
but it's not for sale' and he dropped the chain
of lapis lazuli – blinded blue eyes.
He crouched, his clothes swept some ants,
and he brought it out from a cupboard
like delivering a snake,
gave it into my hands. 'What a weight's
in the leather!' He turned over the buckle:
Hammer and sickle. CCCP.
'Bought it off an Afghani.'
He put it away while the fans overhead
sliced the air, as hot as your breath.

II. KARAKORAM HIGHWAY

*I tuck'd my trowser-ends in my boots and went
and had a good time*
WALT WHITMAN

Stop thinking now, and put on your shoes.
Those cobwebs below, sprinkled with dew:
those are the villages. You
are a blip in someone's long night.
About to be born. Into the light.
Set your watches, we're falling.
There's no friction in flying or thinking ahead.
Wheels have engaged, scorched on the runway
So it's going to be hot, is it? All coming true.

I have seen the devil; he was baking chapati
in an all night roadhouse on the Karakoram Highway.
Flames in his hair, a pit oven, a hook.
Soft talking somnolent takers of tea
and a three-legged dog. Hissing of lanterns
incensed by night. Angora blackness!
Trucks at the roadside, patient and glinting.
Engines revving, our bus backs out,
tinkles, sways. Give the devil his due, let's be going.

The most vivid dream from the darkest sleep:
our headlamps glare on a tanker's rump, all painted
with a trucker's idyll. Green concupiscent hills
trailing in rivers, lazy sun, and one truck,
this one, back-end painted with a trucker's idyll..
we overtake, throwing up dust in the tanker's face.

Shaken down. A grotto-bus.
Jocular groans, the chuckling of the damned, the stoned
absorbed in fairy-lights, intense designs,
luminous bells, talismen,
Aladdin's cavern of rucksacks and ice axes.
Other buses squeeze past like fat rouged tarts
in chrome tiaras,
full of oddly angled limbs, charmed lives;
nothing so Asian as night.

The tailor alone with his sewing machine,
roadside caffs, rows of lit up shacks, silver
stitches in the cloth of night.
Men who'll never meet have seen
our bus, it filled a moment
like the vision on the tanker; or perhaps
they're sustaining us, handing us
each to the next as they look up, look down
at their nocturnal metal work, or basketry.

'Who's the ethnic hitch-hiker?'
'Huh?'
'The Holy Man, the Extra One up front…'
(Bald and brown as a baking bean, he swivels round.)
'Beats me.' 'Psst…
we're taking him to visit his son, in hospital,
just a mile or so…'
'At three a.m.?'
'Fux-ache!'

The wave breaks on the smallest stone,
rolls on. Dawn as eternal occurrence;
always some place. Darkness, dusk, day,
seem immutable as the poplar trees
that make a place. It's permanent
midnight at that check-point, or where
the herd and goats turned to stare
forever half-light, soft as chicks.
Unmanned border of night and day, we rumble on
toward the sun – a tiny cut in orange peel,
sharp sting of smell – Ah, breakfast!

At the sharp end of the gorge;
the bridge. Like a single written word
on vast and rumpled parchment. Bridge.
The statement of man in landscape.

And how they guard it.
Drifts of people in either bank
like brackets, knowing it can crash
to the river in a mangled scribble
and be erased.
They write it up again, single syllable
of construction
shouted over the canyon.

And all the driver wants is eye-drops
before he·straightens up the bus, commits us.
At least malevolence concedes your existence;
worse is indifference, power and indifference.
The river brawls beneath us, self-obsessed,
narcissistic. Wheels turn, turn again, full weight.
The bridge starts to undulate and we're hanging
out of windows half-roads over the Indus,
grinning at each other, impotent, enlightened.
The world grew tight.

It must have been about then we first saw the mountains.

Emotion is human, the foothills brown,
the valley floor very low. We haven't slept.
Our thoughts are slow and wide.
The mind can turn its own death in its hand,
chat blythly about mountains, until
the last moment, that appalling rise that ends
in total unemotional blue.
First sight of the summits, distant
and almost transparent, like glass.
Call it distance, not menace. White, not frightening:
emotion is human, is returned to the human
along with your life. A slight
clash of terror, you lower your eyes.
The sun reflected from glass,
more fearsome than glass in itself.

It's earthly and brown, deep inside canyons.
Stones at the roadside:
'Here rock fell on men', 'men fell to the river'
and the river and rock were unmoved
being river and rock.
He takes it fast.
Some nameless white mountain
has closed off the end of the canyon.
The walls grow taller, the river hysterical.
He brakes, hauls the wheel. No talking.
No colour but brown –
except in the mind. It's been many hours.
Fear passes out into long passive blue,
a slight smile – there is nothing at all we can do.
And the sky widens, the canyon gives out
to a strange sort of kingdom
and the first hanging village swings in.

The year's greening crop spilled
down dull unaltering rock like the tail
of a bird. We can recognise this:

that crops yellow, get cut,
turn in on themselves over winter, head under wing,
and begin to feel like ourselves again.

Suspended villages, terraces
layered wide in the movement of scythes,
the unthreatening gesture of sowing.

Maybe this is as close as we'll get to the mountains.

Squatting on the steps of the K2 Motel
another wretched K2 cigarette.
No great altitude. Clouds sit like headaches
on the walls of this desolate vast arena,
gather round like the Skardu men
with chapati-hats, their clothes
come through dust-storms down the bazaar.

Someone's cooking. The bus has turned back.
Silence and space fall strangely on us all;
leaned against walls with the gear.
Some look at the finances, some at a half-baked
patch of grass, waiting for food
and the day after tomorrow.

Some just look at the hills, keep looking,
tapping plastic spoons onto plastic plates.

That day was raised, a song of a note
from the clapped-out engine. Headwind, hot
in our eyes. Streams, children
splashing down to the roadside, wave,
flowers jammed into their hands 'K2 going?' and
the corn is yellow banked up the hillside.
Lost in dust. This jeep-ride takes us to mountains.

Maybe I'm drowning and this is my life: flashes
on birds' wings, head shaking delight,
beasts in the shade, greenery, embroidery,
women in shawls with the same limbless sway
as a poplar. Grubby babies on roofs, goats,
yaks in a farmyard. Here and passed.
Tree-tips high against blue.
Berries fell to our laps – is this Eden? –
we ate them. Mohammed Ali threw his hat,
caught it, laughed, and
an old dame up an apricot tree
surveyed her river, her valley. High state
of movement, track climbing to meet us
appearing, like everything else at a distance
to blend into heat, to shimmer like mercury.
The shimmer of joy on the face of uncertainty.

The palm of a crystal-gazer's hand
night lifts away, things become defined:
this is our world for a time, these its colours.

Tea fires burn down to embers.
Under the trees they're strapping up baggages,
untying goats. Light fills like a cup

so we pick up our packs and the rhythm of walk.
Keep walking while the world remains sharp
as rock grasped intently,

as the percussion of boots on the track.
While the river's throughout like a sense of myself,
before foot-slogging with thought

gives out to no thought,
to heat and hours mounting like cliffs.
Come noon, we're vacant as goats.

Pain and sun only as undergone.
Until evening, when all things are dismantled:
loads, mountains, trees,

a bit of banter and food,
and we sleep by the track, which continues,
with the sound of the river all night.

Boys drive down the yaks from high pasture
secure them with latches. Darkness comes rising
from rivers, underneath walls
with the light floating up on its back.
Our village rolls itself up in a blanket,
a burst of coughing or song. At length
I untie my boots and leave them outside
under the moon, Orion from home.
Then zip the flaps.
Such fine skin between us and the wide rolling night:
no one feels fearful. Not myself, not the yaks
asleep in their cellars, bovine and black.

Pink bandana slid through his hair
he faces up-river
glances out the corner of slit green eyes.
Holds open the bridge with his foot, his thigh
starts to shudder. The strain, the
sickening river. We come very close.
His clothes are torn, my fingernails bleeding
from clinging to wood.
He slips out his tongue,
parts the two cables an inch more wide
never lowers his eyes.
(Memsahib, you thinking what I..?)

III.

Risk

Your own death smiles out from you.
He is not evil, does not
leer, stink, terrify
old women, old women
are not so easily scared
as young. He is there, unseen, within,
like skeleton.
And in your absence I live alone,
don't keep household ghosts,
I am mistress. But you oscillate
inside my mind
from man to fool to hero to child.
I fear grief, I fear myself
alone with him –
he is a scummy mess we dabble in,
greases our fingers
and stains our hands,
like nicotine.

Things which never shall be

I shall be your wife.
Behind the doors of our house
which are wooden, and plentiful:
dogs and other animals, eager to play.
Rooms of grasses and flowers give out
to further rooms, our house
will be settled among woodland and hills.
So go. And take the dogs with you.
Leave me to work and fecundity in everything:
trees, hedgerows, weather-signs, poetry,
quirks you'll love and mock
only in jest. Our bedroom
will gather bouquets of sunshine,
we'll be home there in winter, I'll play
the spirit and you'll catch your breath.
We'll inhabit a huge place,
where I could move between rooms
with books in my arms,
and our home will be home to all comers.
We'll become skilled in art and endurance,
experts in love, and each other.

Jane

'Would Miss Jane Eyre please report to Airport Information.
Miss Jane Eyre, please.' – heard over P.A. at Heathrow

and he thrust himself into the streams
from every continent – a salmon
shouldering, winding,
searching for a face as pale as chalk.
A bookstore! Surely she'd be there,
peering at the print of worlds she recognised?
No. Nor in the transit lounge
with massive Asian families,
nor the Ladies, weeping beneath
the mounting roar of jets and air-conditioning.
He leaps the stairs – she may be taking
a demure, if plastic, cup of tea –
and surveys the concourse. A dark
hooded bird of prey, he sifts, sifts
the dress of all the nations
for a frock in English grey.
Would he catch her tiny voice
in this damned babble?
The information desk – she shakes her head.
'Shall I page again, Sir?'
He gives a brusque 'No. It was an
off-chance, just an off-chance.'
'Is the lady departing or arriving, Sir,
from where?' But he's striding
from the terminal, and minutes later,
his landrover nudges the northbound carriageway.

Aunt Janet's museum

What can be gained by rushing these things?
Huddle in from the rain, compose ourselves, let
a forefinger rest on the bell button which
requests kindly 'p   s'. We wait, listening
to bus tyres on rain say 'hush' and 'west'.
People hurry behind us, we wait,
for shuffling inside the door,
tumbling locks, and admission to dark.

One after the other we make up the stair.
No one looks back, we know what's there,
fear what lies ahead may disappear. Could we
forget these ritual sounds, or alter their order?
Scuffle of feet on the narrow stair,
the alcove, the turn where
pallid light faints through the glass of the doors.

Let it be right. She takes the handle, still
softly exclaiming over our height, and lets her weight
drop it. The click of the latch. She pushes the door
till the shop bell above gives a delicate ting.
Sounds of inside step forward. The faraway drill
of bells warning the kitchen, and the fallible clock.

Havers

She once went to Girvan on horseback
it's said. Wind from the hillsides
through her hair and its mane, sheep
on the roadside. Havers. Her hair
never felt breezes, caught to her neck
like grey fleece to wire. She appears
and reappears out of the gloom
on her way down to greet us, tiny and silent
as a jet flying through cloud.
How dare we bring inside our knowledge of skies?
We take her hands: saint's bones, kiss her cheek,
thinking of flaky grey parchment
of past summers' wasp-nests,
and hurry to proffer our gift – something blue.

Janet's Armistice

The brown clock drew breath: first stroke of eleven.
Liza burst into tears. Meg almost shouted
'Happy New Year!' as she threw open the window
for the bells and ships' hooters. The street filled,
doors upstairs banged and feet clattered.
Janet finished the filing, neat to the last,
before she reached for her hat. Mr William
stood in his door. 'Thank God it's over.'
He'd lost a son. Then he said 'But the war wasn't won
by singing and dancing. Please, go on with your work.'
The women were standing. Someone was piping
down on the street. Meg glanced at Janet
and clenched her teeth. Liza tried laughing
'It jist disnae matter!'
The boy dragged in some old Jubilee bunting
he'd found in the store. William stared at the floor.
Liza pulled Janet by the sleeve of her suit,
they broke into a run at the door.

Matthew's war

News passed along the pews. Straight from the Kirk
to the hills without changing their suits.
No doubt it was raining. Hands deep in their pockets
and mud on their shiny black shoes, the thing was:
to get there before men from the Ministry.
They strode over the moor, no flat-foots or limping,
five figures in black with their hats on. Now and then
one pointed south at the sky, and they burst into talking.
The German had baled out over Irvine. They took everything
portable, split on the High Street, Jack using a decal
to keep rain off his hat. The pilot's seat came with Matt,
carried in triumph up to his room, where he
dried his bald pate and came so late into dinner
the goose had been picked to the bone.

Orkney haiku

Waves wash in, out, in,
menhirs incline to each other:
farmers grumbling.

A lift from a lobster fisherman!
with red hands. Driving slowly
up and down farm tracks, life on the sea bed.

The latter-day Noah

At last there's industry, heaven-sent work,
batter and clang from the shipyard.
Horses are snorting, pulling in wood, pitch,
hammers. Tell me, what is our cargo?
He nodded out of the window. 'Archetypes.'
And where do we take them? He went on staring.
'Just sail. And keep sailing. Sail over the
edge if you must.' We'll be killed! 'On the contrary
you might find an island.'
With the tigers and sharks?
'I'll send you a sign.' What'll that be?
'A rainbow.' Another arc? You're obsessed!
'You'll all live there forever.'
You mean frogs are immortal?
'The greenfly are...Forms. The cats are not
actual. You must sail to the heavens...' What?
'The transcendent.' But that isn't charted!
'True, but it's near and very like this,'
he said, reaching out to the window,
touching the rain through the glass.

The philosopher extemporises in the fairground

Should we accept the solar system
is, so, in fact, to speak
a Ferris wheel,

(albeit Royal, Televised, Electric and
Noted for Pleasing Young and Old
in Safety and Comfort)

and we are shackled by luck
into this turquoise cart
and here secured

by a tattooed gypsy who
sets the wheel rolling
only to leave

to watch his son walk the nebulous
waltzers, like some casual
Christ on water?

Then. He is neglecting us.
We are slowing down.
Our sky blue vehicle

may well attain that coveted
space, point the highest,
nearest the stars.

We may well sway above
the lurid art
and flashes

and little golden fishes.
Never, however, the less
we thinkers descend

and must assume we will meet
with no greater end than a jerk
of our tinker's thumb.

God Almighty the first garden made

How did I get where I am today?
How did I get where I am today? Lass,
I hauled mesel up by me own boot straps. See
all I started out with was seventeen jars of bluebells,
and were on funerals for years. Then I 'ad this idea...

For fenugreek, and marigolds, then along came the anemones,
down the mart at dawn, I bought in job lots of greenery,
expanded in a small way with a little blend for England,
(hollyhocks and foxgloves and Cox's orange pippins.)

Secured an export deal for cacti, but I got me fingers burned
on nettles. They'd no sooner got laburnum seeds
then they're clamouring for wheat. I gave it, too; albeit
with poppies. (I'm not a hard man, I hear deputations, Sundays)

T'Word spread. Travellers went to Africa with suchlike
samples of exotica as malachite, antelopes, and a tropical strain
of thunder. Then t'was Lapsang Souchong and iridescent bees,
BUT I never forgot me roots, oh no! (Ah me! them Baobab trees!)

I'm getting on. I'll be calling it a day soon,
and handing over to me son. I just fidget
with hedgerows now, do a small line in peas. I like
to put me feet up on me footstool, sunny afternoons,
and cut me own toenails to meet demand for crescent moons.

Petrol

Sketch in the background: pre-dawn
in winter, snow on the hillsides,
marsh: brown-green, a winding
lochside road,
black ice.

It could have been
so much worse. No one was hurt.
As if you can care about
alternative universes
when this one gives trouble enough. O

that bonny smashed-up power-steering,
disc-brakes, axle,
front nearside suspension; no more
easy overnighting, end
of spinning our cash into petrol.

We must haul ourselves
out of the mire with help
from the keeper's tractor and none
whatsoever from the governors of fate,
who look down

on the scratch-marks, and smile.
Who look down on the petrol
spilled on the roadside
and smile.
It's business. It's tough.

The engine we'll resurrect, someday.
Tonight, hit the whisky
till we're split out through the spectrum:
as readily consumed, as volatile,
as figures etched in petrol.

The way we live

Pass the tambourine, let me bash out praises
to the Lord God of movement, to Absolute
non-friction, flight, and the scarey side:
death by avalanche, birth by failed contraception.
Of chicken tandoori and reggae, loud, from tenements,
commitment, driving fast and unswerving
friendship. Of tee-shirts on pulleys, giros and Bombay,
barmen, dreaming waitresses with many fake-gold
bangles. Of airports, impulse, and waking to uncertainty,
to strip-lights, motorways, or that pantheon –
the mountains. To overdrafts and grafting

and the fit slow pulse of wipers as you're
creeping over Rannoch, while the God of moorland
walks abroad with his entourage of freezing fog,
his bodyguard of snow.
Of endless gloaming in the North, of Asiatic swelter,
to launderettes, anecdotes, passions and exhaustion,
Final Demands and dead men, the skeletal grip
of government. To misery and elation; mixed,
the sod and caprice of landlords.
To the way it fits, the way it is, the way it seems
to be: let me bash out praises – pass the tambourine.